L

 **Specific Skill Series**
for Reading

Using Phonics

Sixth Edition

Columbus, OH

The **McGraw·Hill** Companies

SRAonline.com

Copyright © 2006 by SRA/McGraw-Hill.

Printed in the United States of America.

Send all inquiries to:
SRA/McGraw-Hill
8787 Orion Place
Columbus, OH 43240-4027

ISBN 0-07-603972-2

1 2 3 4 5 6 7 8 9 BCH 12 11 10 09 08 07 06 05

PURPOSE:

USING PHONICS helps students put sounds and other word elements to work to determine word meaning. Many units in **USING PHONICS** develop understanding about sound-symbol (phonic) associations. Other units address letter combinations, syllabication, prefixes and suffixes, compound words, longer words, and spelling changes caused by adding endings.

FOR WHOM:

The skill of **USING PHONICS** is developed through a series of books spanning five levels (Picture, Preparatory, A, B, C). The Picture Level is for students who have not acquired a basic sight vocabulary. The Preparatory Level is for students who have a basic sight vocabulary but are not yet ready for the first-grade-level book. Books A through C are appropriate for students who can read on levels one through three, respectively.

THE NEW EDITION:

The sixth edition of the ***Specific Skill Series for Reading*** maintains the quality and focus that has distinguished this program for more than 40 years. A key element central to the program's success has been the unique nature of the reading selections. Fiction and nonfiction pieces about current topics have been designed to stimulate the interest of students, motivating them to use the comprehension strategies they have learned to further their reading. To keep this important aspect of the program intact, a percentage of the reading selections has been replaced in order to ensure the continued relevance of the subject material.

In addition, a significant percentage of the artwork in the program has been replaced to give the books a contemporary look. The cover photographs are designed to appeal to readers of all ages.

SESSIONS:

Short practice sessions are the most effective. It is desirable to have a practice session every day or every other day, using a few units each session.

SCORING:

Students should record their answers on the reproducible worksheets. The worksheets make scoring easier and provide uniform records of the students' work. Using worksheets also avoids consuming the exercise books.

It is important for students to know how well they are doing. For this reason, units should be scored as soon as they have been completed. Then a discussion can be held in which students justify their choices. (The *Language Activity Pages,* many of which are open-ended, do not lend themselves to an objective score; thus there are no answer keys for these pages.)

GENERAL INFORMATION ON *USING PHONICS:*

The units are of two types: concept builders and functional exercises. The concept units focus the reader's attention on common patterns and parts of words. Each generalization is built step-by-step on the structure of previously formed concepts. The functional exercises either follow the concept units or are contained within them. They provide the reader with many immediate and repeated experiences with words involving particular patterns or principles. Sentence settings are typical for the students' level; often the choices offered are new words.

As **USING PHONICS** progresses through different word elements, constant reinforcement is occurring. The more elementary booklets focus on phonic elements such as consonant sounds, consonant substitutions, blends, phonograms, and vowel sounds. As the level of difficulty increases, the emphasis shifts to syllabication, prefixes, suffixes, and roots.

A unit-by-unit list of concepts developed in this book is found on page 64.

INSTRUCTIONS:

Minimal direction is required. Students' attention must be drawn to the answer choices. In the concept units only two or three answer choices are offered. In the units that provide application of understandings, four to nine answer choices are offered, providing more experiences with words of a particular pattern. In units that offer an *F* choice, the *F* stands for NONE. This means that none of the choices makes sense in that particular setting.

RELATED MATERIALS:

Specific Skill Series Assessment Book provides the teacher with a pretest and a posttest for each skill at each grade level. These tests will help the teacher assess the students' performance in each of the nine comprehension skills.

One of the first things you learned in school was the alphabet. You know the name of each letter in the alphabet. You know that written words are made of these letters.

As you learn to read, you learn the sounds that letters stand for in words. First, you look at the letters in a word. Next, you put together the sounds of the letters. Then, you can tell what the word is.

You can think of a word as a kind of secret message written in code. You are a spy trying to find the meaning of that secret message. You are trying to **decode** the word. The sounds the letters stand for are the key to unlocking the code.

In this book, you will look at four pictures on a page. You will say the name for each picture. Then you will read four sentences. Each sentence has a blank. The word that goes in the blank is the name of one of the pictures. For some pages, the letter that stands for the **first** sound in the picture name is given as a clue. For other pages, the letter that stands for the **last** sound in the picture name is given as a clue. The word *monkey* begins with the letter *m*. The word *leaf* ends with the letter *f*. If you know the sounds that letters stand for, you will get the right answers.

When you know the sounds that letters stand for, you will have a key to reading. You will be able to unlock the meaning of written words.

1. The **m**____ likes to run.

2. We will go into the **t**____.

3. Jenny fixed the rip with **t**____.

4. Look in the **m**____.

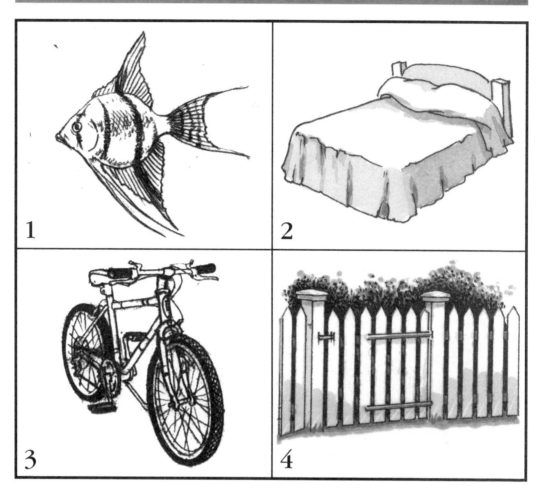

1. Dad went to **b____**.

_____

2. The **f____** is in the water.

_____

3. Can you jump the **f____**?

_____

4. I can ride a **b____**.

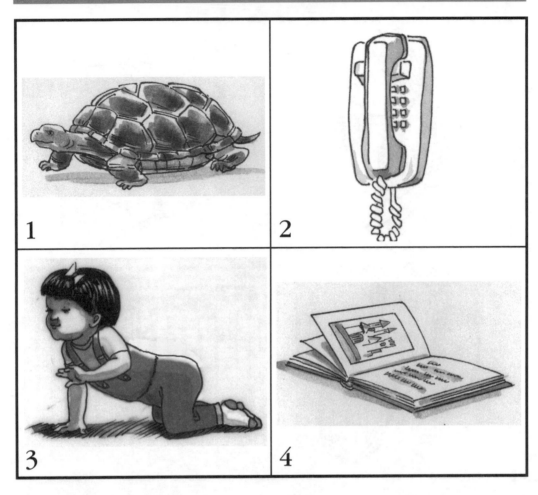

1. Ella has a pet **t**_____.

_____

2. She is a little **b**_____.

_____

3. Call me on the **t**_____.

_____

4. I read a good **b**_____.

1. We can go play **f**___.

2. Do not play with **m**___.

3. The **f**___ will make me feel cool.

4. Dad is a big **m**___.

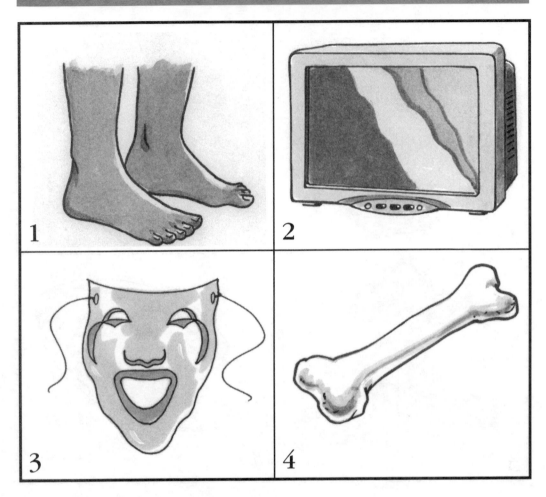

1. Bill likes to watch **t**____.

_____

2. Your **f**____ are wet.

_____

3. The **b**____ is for my dog.

_____

4. That is a funny **m**____.

1. Berto is in the **h____**.

2. Can you walk up that **h____**?

3. Mom has a new **c____**.

4. May I have a **c____**?

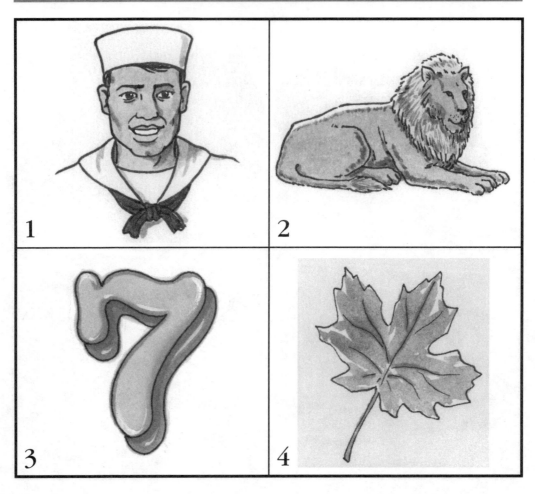

1. I saw a **l___** at the zoo.

_____

2. That man is a **s___**.

_____

3. There are **s___** balls in the box.

_____

4. The **l___** is green.

1. She can ride a **h**___.

2. Dion is on a **l**___.

3. Ken has a new **h**___.

4. I will read the **l**___.

1. My **c**____ ran away.

_____

2. I have one **s**____.

_____

3. Can you read the **s**____?

_____

4. May I eat the **c**____?

1. Mom hit the nail with a **h**___.

2. Akayo sat on a **l**___.

3. My **c**___ is too big.

4. Put the **s**___ in the water.

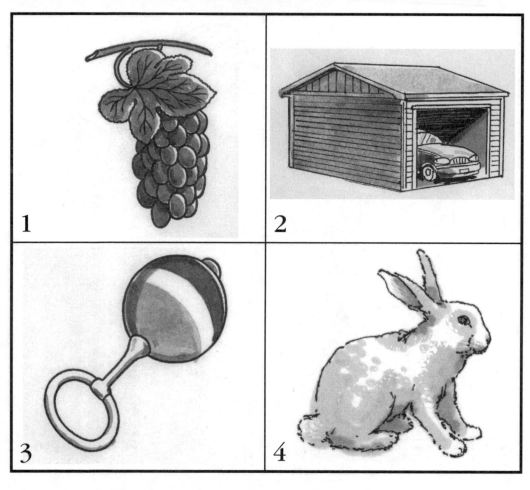

1. The car is in the **g**____.

2. The baby has a new **r**____.

3. Mom gave me some **g**____.

4. Ann has a pet **r**____.

1. Can you play the **p**____?

2. I am going to eat the **p**____.

3. Look out the **w**____.

4. Come ride in my **w**____.

A. Exercising Your Skill

Name each picture below. Listen to the beginning sound. Say the letter that stands for the beginning sound.

| Say one word that names something in a kitchen and begins with the same sound as the thing in picture 1. | Say one word that names something in a kitchen and begins with the same sound as the thing in picture 2. |

B. Expanding Your Skill

Work with a partner. See how many things you can name that go in a kitchen. Say their names or draw them.

C. Exploring Language

Make alphabet soup. Look at the circle and the letters inside it. Then add these letters in the correct spots to make food names:

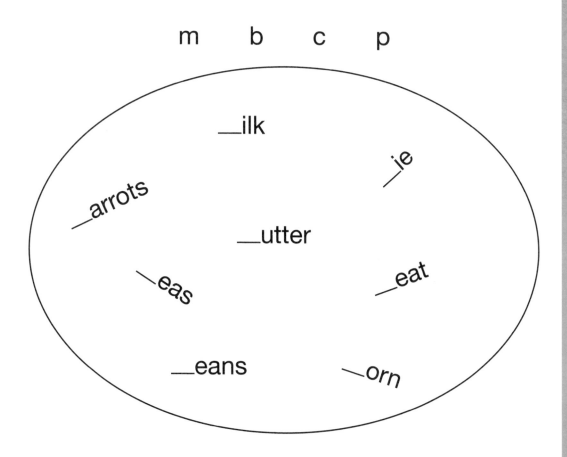

m   b   c   p

_ilk

_arrots

_ie

_utter

_eas

_eat

_eans

_orn

D. Expressing Yourself

Share a recipe with a friend. Pick something you like to eat. Tell all the things you need to make it. Then tell how to make it.

1. A **w**____ came to my house.

2. A car went down the **r**____.

3. Sam got wet in the **r**____.

4. Paint the **w**____ blue.

1. Eva worked in the **g**____.

2. Put the **p**____ on the bed.

3. That **g**____ can read.

4. Put some water in the **p**____.

1. Can you wear that **r**____?

2. She has a new **w**____.

3. The **p**____ likes to eat.

4. That is a big **g**____.

1. Please ring the **d**____.

2. He is a **k**____.

3. We eat in the **k**____.

4. A **d**____ can run fast.

1. Grandpa likes to read the **n**____.

2. That is a sharp **n**____.

3. Wash your hands in the **s**____.

4. For lunch I had a **s**____.

1. Kayla's pet is a **k**___.

2. A **n**___ is in the tree.

3. **N**___ boys played ball.

4. I have a **k**___ to my house.

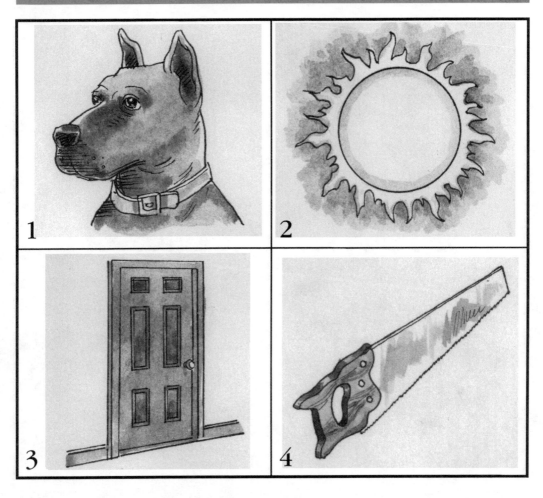

1. My **d**___ is named Jake.

_____

2. Dan works with a **s**___.

_____

3. What is behind that **d**___?

_____

4. The **s**___ is far away.

1. Meg likes to eat **s**____.

_____

2. A **k**____ is at the zoo.

_____

3. Mom gave me a new **d**____.

_____

4. My **n**____ is cold.

1. Jill has a pet **m**____.

2. The **c**____ can go fast.

3. Put on your **c**____.

4. That **m**____ has a boat.

1. My **h**___ is painted green.

2. The book is on the **t**___.

3. I like your **h**___ and coat.

4. Did you hear the **t**___?

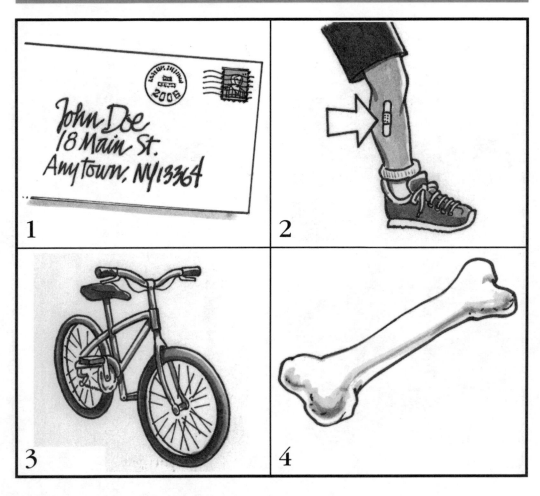

1. May I read your **l**____?

_____

2. Did you cut your **l**____?

_____

3. My dog chews on that **b**____.

_____

4. Nora has a new **b**____.

1. They put out the **f**____.

_____

2. Clean with **s**____ and water.

_____

3. Grandma made **s**____ to eat.

_____

4. Tom ran with the **f**____.

A. Exercising Your Skill

Look at the pictures. Add the missing letter to each sentence.

I go to school on a
____us.
I take a seat near the
____ack.

I sit at my ____esk.
It is by the ____oor.

B. Expanding Your Skill

Play I Spy. Think of the name of a thing in the room. Tell the beginning sound. See who can guess what word you are thinking of. Give one point for each correct guess.

Use these beginning sounds:

| b | l | w | g | n | s | c | t |

C. Exploring Language

Add the missing letters to complete the story. Then think of one more sentence you could add.

Our teacher told a tale.
It was such a ___illy story!
It was about a pink ___ig named Pete.
He ran into our ___oom.
He had a hat on his ___ead.
He had big blue ___oots on his feet.

D. Expressing Yourself

Draw a picture of the animal in the story above. Give the picture a name.

1. The **d**____ on the house is new.

2. The car is in the **g**____.

3. Do you know that **g**____?

4. My **d**____ is hungry.

1. Elan's **k**___ likes to play.

2. This **r**___ goes to my house.

3. Can you fly a **k**___?

4. Look at the **r**___ jump.

1. Juan painted the **w**___ blue.

2. That **w**___ is my mom.

3. Did you read the **n**___?

4. I have **n**___ books.

1. Put on your blue **s**____.

_____

2. That **p**____ is fat.

_____

3. What is in the **p**____?

_____

4. Tell me what the **s**____ says.

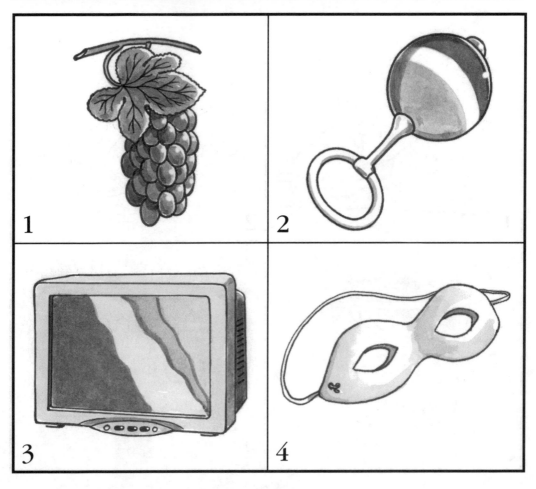

1. Who gave the baby the **r**____?

_____

2. Put on the funny **m**____.

_____

3. The **g**____ are sweet.

_____

4. We have a new **t**____.

1. Look at the **k**____.

_____

2. May I have some **p**___?

_____

3. Turn on the **f**___.

_____

4. The house is made of **w**___.

1. The **d**___ can run fast.

2. I have a pet **c**___.

3. He can ride a **h**___.

4. Do not jump on the **b**___.

1. The man put on his **v**____.

2. We saw a lion at the **z**____.

3. That woman is the **qu**____.

4. I like to play with the **y**____.

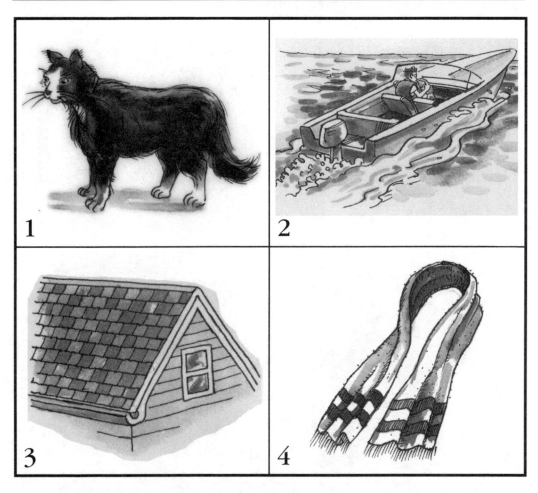

1. May I ride in the ___t?

_____

2. That house has a new ___f.

_____

3. Put on your ___f.

_____

4. My ___t jumped on my bed.

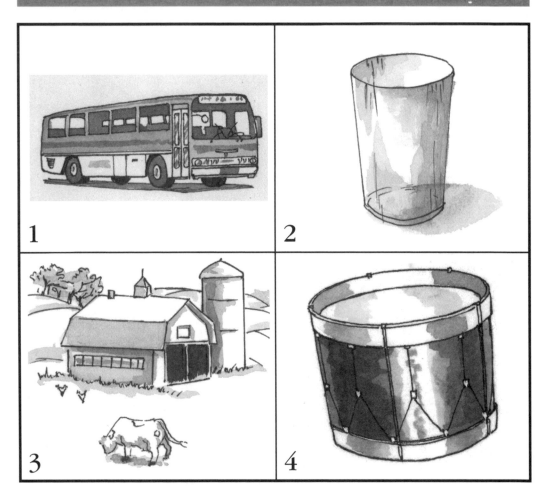

1. I saw cows at the ____m.

_____

2. Mom rides on a ____s.

_____

3. Can you play that ____m?

_____

4. Fill the ____s with milk.

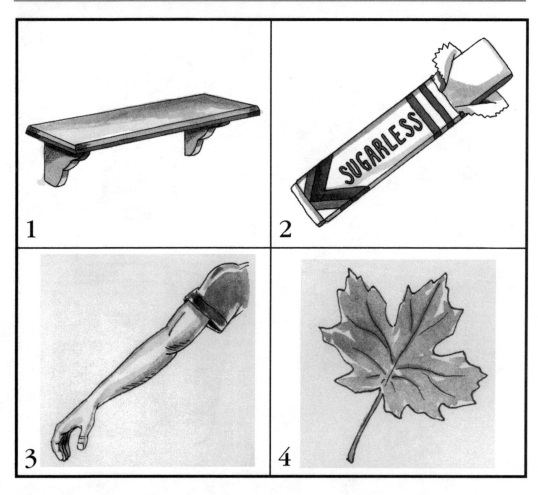

1. Put the book on the ___f.

2. This ___f is from that tree.

3. Do not eat the ___m.

4. Did he fall and cut his ___m?

1. Put it in the ＿＿t.

2. Try on your new ＿＿s.

3. Do not fall down the ＿＿s.

4. The ＿＿t is Imani's pet.

1. I saw Jun on the ____s.

2. My cat is on the ____f.

3. We stayed in a ____t.

4. The fish ate the ____m.

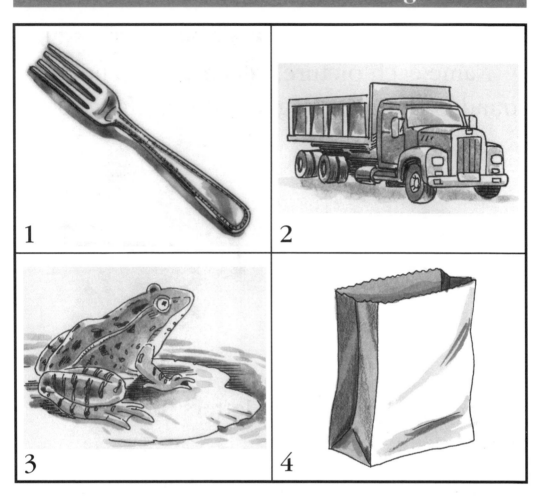

1. My pet ___**g** can jump far.

2. I will eat this with a ___**k.**

3. I have a ___**g** of toys.

4. Did you ride in the ___**k?**

A. Exercising Your Skill

Name each picture. Listen to the ending sound. Say the missing letter in each word.

ca___   do___

Now add the missing letters to make animal names.

I am bigger than a mouse. I am a ra___.
I can wiggle in the dirt. I am a wor___.
I swim and I fly. I am a duc___.

B. Expanding Your Skill

Think of an animal name. Now think of as many other animal names as you can that have the same beginning sound. Share your names with a classmate.

C. Exploring Language

Read these sentences. Say the missing letters.

A fro___ can hop on a log.
A ___orse can kic___ with its hoofs.
A snake can his___, but it cannot kis___.
A ___ird can tweet a sweet song.
A pi___ grows very big.

D. Expressing Yourself

Do one of these things.

1. Sing "Old MacDonald Had a Farm." When you get to the name of a new animal, say only the beginning sound. Let your classmates guess its name.

2. Draw and color four animals. Cut them apart. See if a classmate can put the heads and tails back together.

1. A ___p is a big boat.

2. That cat has a long ___l.

3. This ___l is for a wagon.

4. I saw a ___p at the zoo.

1. A ___l ran up the tree.

2. Look at the ___g eat.

3. The girls played ___l.

4. The baby played on the ___g.

1. Bob sat at his ___k.

2. Can you open this ___k?

3. Put the ___p on the table.

4. Clean the floor with a ___p.

1. May I eat the ___**g?**

_____

2. We have a new ___**p.**

_____

3. Mom walked down the ___**l.**

_____

4. A ___**k** tells time.

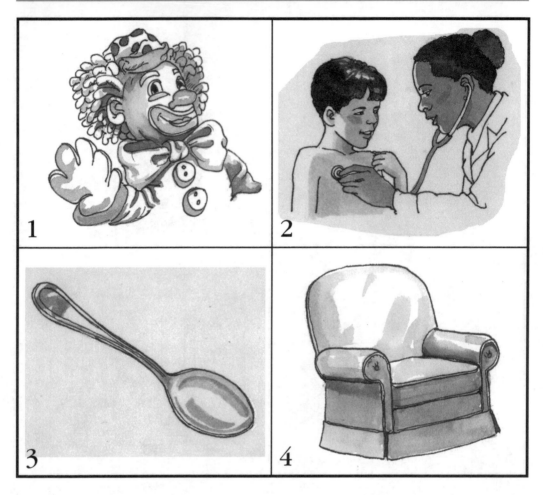

1. She is a ____r.

_____

2. The ____n is funny.

_____

3. The baby eats with a ____n.

_____

4. Sit on the ____r.

1. My house is made of ___**d.**

2. A ___**k** likes the rain.

3. He got a new ___**d.**

4. May I read your ___**k?**

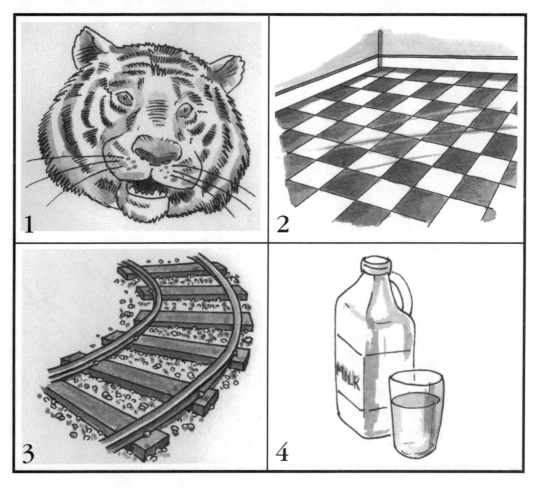

1. Give the baby some ___**k.**

2. The boys sat on the ___**r.**

3. That ___**r** is not a pet.

4. Put the train on the ___**k.**

1. We have ___**n** books.

2. The potatoes are in the ___**n.**

3. I see a ___**d** in the tree.

4. Put the ___**d** on the pot.

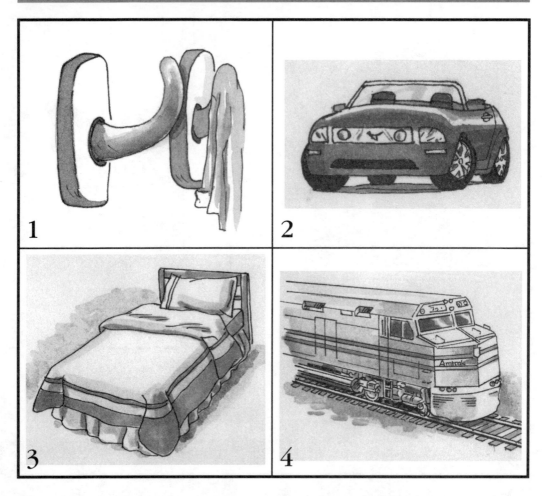

1. The ___**r** went down the road.

2. Do not jump on your ___**d**.

3. The coat is on a ___**k**.

4. Trina has a toy ___**n**.

1. See the baby ___**k!**

2. The ___**t** is big.

3. You have a little ___**g.**

4. Marcos has a new ___**f.**

1. May I have some ___d?

_____

2. Put the toys in the ___x.

_____

3. Who has my ___m?

_____

4. Will you go up that ___r?

1. May I play with your ___l?

2. We looked at the ___p.

3. Hiro has a pet ___k.

4. The cows are in the ___n.

A. Exercising Your Skill

Read these signs that go on a road. Think about the ending sounds. Add the missing letters.

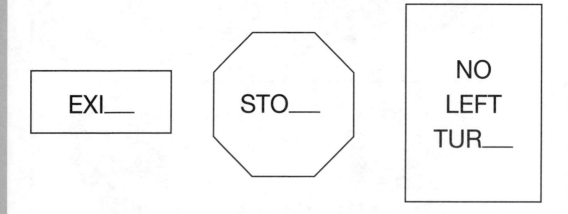

EXI___

STO___

NO
LEFT
TUR___

B. Expanding Your Skill

Make a list of other signs you have seen. Think about signs on roads, signs at school, and signs on stores.

Say the name of each sign, but leave the last letter off each one. See if your classmates can add the correct letter.

Compare your signs with those of your classmates. How many different ones do you have in all?

C. Exploring Language

Look at the arrows. Add the ending sound to each word to show what the arrows mean.

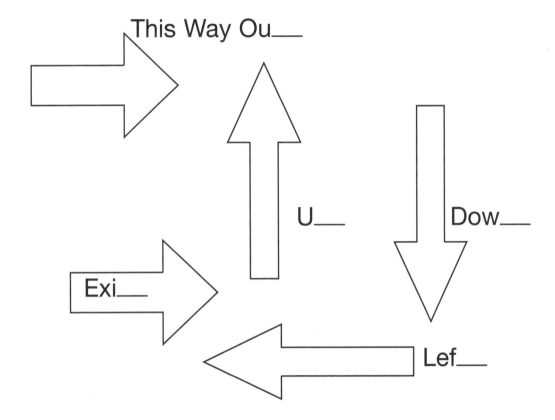

This Way Ou__

U__

Dow__

Exi__

Lef__

D. Expressing Yourself

Draw and color a sign you have seen. Think about why we need this sign. Tell your class about it.

Concepts Developed